A Den in the Woods

by Catherine Baker

OXFORD
UNIVERSITY PRESS

You can visit the woods in summer. It is fun!

Den

Put up a den in the woods.

Look for a low fork.

an oak fork

an ash fork

a willow fork

Pick tall bits of wood.
Pop them upright in the fork.

Push the shoots and ferns in.
This will keep the rain off.

The den is secure!
Now you can sit in it.

Patterns

Turn things in the wood into art.
Look at the patterns.

Look for it!

oak

ash

beech

willow

Rocks, moss and nutshells are good, too.
What patterns can you think of?

Footmarks

Look for animal footmarks in the woods.

You might see rabbit, fox or otter footmarks.

rabbit

fox

otter

You can put footmarks in the mud!

When will you visit the woods?
What will you see and hear?

You can rub bark to get patterns!

1. Put the sheet on the bark.

2. Rub the bark.

3. See the pattern form.

  Read through the steps together. Have a go at a bark rubbing the next time you go out.